MW01093895

$\mathcal{S}$PIRITUAL $\mathcal{W}$ARFARE

JOURNAL

**MODERN
ENGLISH
VERSION**

CONTENTS

INTRODUCTION

THERE IS MORE to life than meets the eye. Beneath the surface of our daily routines and challenges lies a spiritual reality—a battlefield where forces of good and evil contend for influence over our lives, our relationships, and our purpose. This unseen conflict is what we call spiritual warfare.

Though the concept may seem daunting or mysterious, it is not meant to evoke fear but rather to inspire readiness. Scripture assures us that as believers in Christ we are not helpless in this fight. We have been given tools, weapons, and divine authority to stand firm against any attack of the enemy and walk in victory.

This journal is designed to be a companion in your journey, providing you with wisdom, encouragement, and practical guidance to engage in spiritual warfare effectively. Use its pages to build a deeper understanding of God's Word, recognize the enemy's strategies, and grow stronger in faith as you stand firm in the armor of God.

Spiritual warfare is not a solitary endeavor; it is an invitation to draw closer to God and rely fully on His grace. It is not a battle you fight alone but one where Christ has already secured the ultimate victory.

As you engage with this journal, take time to record what the Holy Spirit is speaking to you through His Word. Write down the insights, encouragement, and strategies He reveals, and use the "Battle Plans and Breakthroughs" section to track your prayer strategies and record your victories.

Gratitude is a powerful tool in spiritual warfare, strengthening your faith as you remember what God has done. So thank Him for answered prayers—both seen and unseen—trusting that He is always working on your behalf.

The battle is real, but so is your victory. May these pages equip, empower, and embolden you to stand firm, pray boldly, and move forward in faith.

THE GREATEST ENEMY

THE GREATEST ENEMY of the church is not sin but ignorance. Satan's number one goal is to keep you ignorant concerning the kingdom, as was described in Hosea 4:6: "My people are destroyed for lack of knowledge." Even as Satan challenged Jesus in Matthew 4, so it is today with the church. The key issue has to do with the kingdom, because it is literally God's rule on the earth through man—His earthly representatives.

Think about that for a moment. What rules heaven? God's will as expressed in His laws and principles. Is there sickness in heaven? No. Is there poverty in heaven? No. Is there slavery, sex trafficking, drug and alcohol abuse, oppression, famine, war, child soldiers, persecution, terrorism, malnutrition, bankruptcy, or water that isn't safe to drink in heaven? No. The things that are tearing our world apart don't exist in heaven, because God's will is as accessible there as breathing the air is to us.

As long as man does not take his rightful stance, posture, and place in God through prayer, evil and evil human beings will rule. Herein lies the challenge. You must arise and take your place so that through you God can restore order, peace, righteousness, morality, ethics, just governance, health, and healing.

God planted within each of us a desire to make a difference in our world—to bring good and not harm, peace and not strife, prosperity and not poverty. But too few realize that the groundwork for this overcoming lifestyle begins in the prayer closet. It is the place of training and preparation. It is the boot camp to overcoming.

There are battles still raging for the peoples of the earth, and those battles are fought in the spiritual realm before they manifest in the natural. The Spirit realm is the causal realm. If you prevail in the Spirit, you will win in the natural. If you can learn the art of victory through intercession, then such struggles that steal the souls of humanity need not ever manifest at all.

—CINDY TRIMM, *THE ART OF WAR FOR SPIRITUAL BATTLE*

WHAT IS THE LORD SPEAKING TO YOU?

_____

_____

_____

_____

_____

_____

_____

_____

_____

_____

_____

Finally, my brothers, be strong in the Lord
and in the power of His might. Put on the
whole armor of God that you may be able
to stand against the schemes of the devil.

—EPHESIANS 6:10–11

_____

_____

_____

_____

_____

_____

_____

_____

_____

_____

BATTLE PLANS AND BREAKTHROUGHS

WHAT IS THE LORD SPEAKING TO YOU?

_____

_____

_____

_____

_____

_____

_____

_____

_____

_____

> You must not be frightened of them, for the
> LORD your God is among you, a great and
> awesome God. The LORD your God will drive
> out those nations before you, little by little.
> You will not be able to destroy them all at
> once, lest the beasts of the field become too
> numerous for you. But the LORD your God will
> deliver them to you and will throw them into
> a great confusion until they are destroyed.
>
> —DEUTERONOMY 7:21–23

_____

_____

_____

_____

_____

_____

_____

_____

_____

BATTLE PLANS AND BREAKTHROUGHS

WHAT IS THE LORD SPEAKING TO YOU?

_____

_____

_____

_____

_____

_____

_____

_____

_____

_____

_____

For though we walk in the flesh, we do not
war according to the flesh. For the weapons
of our warfare are not carnal, but mighty
through God for the pulling down of strongholds, casting down arguments and every
high thing that exalts itself against the
knowledge of God, bringing every thought
into captivity to the obedience of Christ.

—2 CORINTHIANS 10:3–5

_____

_____

_____

_____

_____

_____

_____

_____

_____

_____

Battle Plans and Breakthroughs

WHAT IS THE LORD SPEAKING TO YOU?

_____

_____

_____

_____

_____

_____

_____

_____

_____

_____

_____

Your right hand, O LORD, is glorious in power.
Your right hand, O LORD, shatters the enemy.
In the greatness of Your excellence, You over-
throw those who rise up against You. You send
out Your wrath; it consumes them like stubble.

—EXODUS 15:6–7

_____

_____

_____

_____

_____

_____

_____

_____

_____

BATTLE PLANS AND BREAKTHROUGHS

DATE:

WHAT IS THE LORD SPEAKING TO YOU?

_____

_____

_____

_____

_____

_____

_____

_____

_____

_____

Surely He shall deliver you from the snare of
the fowler and from the deadly pestilence. He
shall cover you with His pinions, and under
His wings shall you find refuge; His faith-
fulness shall be your shield and buckler.

—PSALM 91:3–4

10

BATTLE PLANS AND BREAKTHROUGHS

WHAT IS THE LORD SPEAKING TO YOU?

_____

_____

_____

_____

_____

_____

_____

_____

_____

_____

No weapon that is formed against you shall
prosper, and every tongue that shall rise against
you in judgment, you shall condemn. This is
the inheritance of the servants of the LORD, and
their vindication is from Me, says the LORD.

—ISAIAH 54:17

_____

_____

_____

_____

_____

_____

_____

_____

_____

Battle Plans and Breakthroughs

WHAT IS THE LORD SPEAKING TO YOU?

_____

_____

_____

_____

_____

_____

_____

_____

_____

_____

_____

You are of God, little children, and have
overcome them, because He who is in you
is greater than he who is in the world.

—1 JOHN 4:4

_____

_____

_____

_____

_____

_____

_____

_____

_____

BATTLE PLANS AND BREAKTHROUGHS

WHAT IS THE LORD SPEAKING TO YOU?

_____

_____

_____

_____

_____

_____

_____

_____

_____

_____

_____

I can do all things, because of
Christ who strengthens me.

—PHILIPPIANS 4:13

_____

_____

_____

_____

_____

_____

_____

_____

_____

BATTLE PLANS AND
BREAKTHROUGHS

DATE:

WHAT IS THE LORD SPEAKING TO YOU?

_____

_____

_____

_____

_____

_____

_____

_____

_____

_____

Therefore submit yourselves to God. Resist the devil, and he will flee from you. Draw near to God, and He will draw near to you.

—JAMES 4:7–8

18

_____

_____

_____

_____

_____

_____

_____

_____

BATTLE PLANS AND BREAKTHROUGHS

DATE:

WHAT IS THE LORD SPEAKING TO YOU?

_____

_____

_____

_____

_____

_____

_____

_____

_____

_____

> But thanks be to God, who gives us the victory through our Lord Jesus Christ!
>
> —1 CORINTHIANS 15:57

20

_____

_____

_____

_____

_____

_____

_____

_____

_____

_____

Battle Plans and Breakthroughs

DATE:

WHAT IS THE LORD SPEAKING TO YOU?

_____

_____

_____

_____

_____

_____

_____

_____

_____

_____

Be strong and of a good courage. Fear
not, nor be afraid of them, for the LORD
your God, it is He who goes with you. He
will not fail you, nor forsake you.

—DEUTERONOMY 31:6

_____

_____

_____

_____

_____

_____

_____

_____

_____

BATTLE PLANS AND BREAKTHROUGHS

THE WEAPONS OF OUR WARFARE

IF A MILITARY is going to win a war, they must know how to use their weapons, and it is no different in spiritual warfare. We have been well equipped for this battle, and there are many weapons made available to us.

Prayer

Prayer is the key to effective spiritual warfare. Prayer releases God's flow into your life so you can defeat the enemy. It is a two-way communication system whereby you communicate with God and God communicates with you. If we become weak during the battle, prayer links us into God's strength, especially when we pray in the spirit. Prayer is also the surest way to receive God's instructions and to lean upon His infinite wisdom.

Fasting

Fasting is a spiritual discipline that increases our prayer power. It humbles the soul and gives us the ability to become laser sharp in our spiritual walk with God. Mark 9:29 tells us that sometimes gaining the victory over certain tactics of the enemy can come through only prayer and fasting. Isaiah 58:6–9 talks about fasting also being a means of loosing the bands of wickedness, oppression, yokes, affliction, poverty, and sadness.

Faith

Matthew 21:22 and 1 John 5:4 tell us that our faith is what ensures our victory over the god of this world and it guarantees that what we ask to be delivered from, healed of, and empowered for will be done.

The blood of Jesus

Through the shed blood of Jesus Christ, we have already won and overcome all the forces of the enemy. Revelation 12:11 says, "They overcame him by the blood of the Lamb and by the word of their testimony."

The Word of God

In Ephesians 6 we find the spiritual armor that we are to gird ourselves with. Verse 17 talks about one of the most formidable weapons we have access to—the Word of God, which is referred to in this text as "the sword of the Spirit." The sword of the Spirit enables us to quickly and keenly discern spirits, thoughts, and intents (Heb. 4:12).

The person and name of Jesus

With Jesus dwelling in us, we are greater than any power at work in the world (1 John 4:4). Philippians 2:9–11 also tells us that the name of Jesus is above every name and "that at the name of Jesus every knee should bow, of those in heaven and on earth and under the earth, and every tongue should confess that Jesus Christ is Lord."

The anointing

According to Isaiah 10:27, every burden that is on our shoulders and every yoke around our necks will be destroyed by the power of the anointing. The anointing is the power, provisions, and presence of God manifested through the person of the Holy Spirit.

Spirit praying

Spirit praying, or more commonly praying in the spirit, is essential in any believer's arsenal of weapons. According to Jude 20, this weapon has the ability to strengthen the inner man. Praying in the spirit also helps us when we don't know what to pray or what is wrong in certain situations. It allows our spirits to pray out directly into the intercession room of the Holy Spirit, where He is able to search our hearts and intercede strategically on our behalf (Rom. 8:26–27).

Praise

Praise is a weapon of warfare. Psalm 149:6–9 says, "Let the high praises of God be in their mouth, and a two-edged sword in their hand, to execute vengeance on the nations...to execute on them the judgment written!" Praise is also God's will for us (1 Thess. 5:18), and when we are walking in the will of God, we are assured victory.

—CINDY TRIMM, *THE RULES OF ENGAGEMENT*

WHAT IS THE LORD SPEAKING TO YOU?

_____

_____

_____

_____

_____

_____

_____

_____

_____

_____

But the Lord is faithful, who will establish you and guard you from the evil one.

—2 THESSALONIANS 3:3

_____

_____

_____

_____

_____

_____

_____

_____

_____

_____

Battle Plans and Breakthroughs

WHAT IS THE LORD SPEAKING TO YOU?

_____

_____

_____

_____

_____

_____

_____

_____

_____

_____

The Lord will deliver me from every evil work
and will preserve me for His heavenly kingdom,
to whom be glory forever and ever. Amen.

—2 TIMOTHY 4:18

_____

_____

_____

_____

_____

_____

_____

_____

_____

BATTLE PLANS AND BREAKTHROUGHS

DATE:

WHAT IS THE LORD SPEAKING TO YOU?

_____

_____

_____

_____

_____

_____

_____

_____

_____

_____

_____

And having disarmed authorities and
powers, He made a show of them openly,
triumphing over them by the cross.

—COLOSSIANS 2:15

_____

_____

_____

_____

_____

_____

_____

_____

_____

BATTLE PLANS AND BREAKTHROUGHS

DATE:

WHAT IS THE LORD SPEAKING TO YOU?

_____

_____

_____

_____

_____

_____

_____

_____

_____

_____

> Because you have made the LORD, who is my
> refuge, even the Most High, your dwelling, no
> evil will befall you, nor will any plague come
> near your tent; for He will give His angels
> charge over you to guard you in all your
> ways. They will bear you up in their hands,
> lest you strike your foot against a stone.
>
> —PSALM 91:9–12

_____

_____

_____

_____

_____

_____

_____

_____

_____

BATTLE PLANS AND BREAKTHROUGHS

WHAT IS THE LORD SPEAKING TO YOU?

_____

_____

_____

_____

_____

_____

_____

_____

_____

_____

_____

Behold, I give you authority to trample
on serpents and scorpions, and over all
the power of the enemy. And nothing
shall by any means hurt you.

—LUKE 10:19

_____

_____

_____

_____

_____

_____

_____

_____

_____

BATTLE PLANS AND
BREAKTHROUGHS

WHAT IS THE LORD SPEAKING TO YOU?

_____

_____

_____

_____

_____

_____

_____

_____

_____

_____

The LORD will cause your enemies who
rise up against you to be defeated before
you; they will come out against you one
way and flee before you seven ways.

—DEUTERONOMY 28:7

_____

_____

_____

_____

_____

_____

_____

_____

_____

BATTLE PLANS AND
BREAKTHROUGHS

WHAT IS THE LORD SPEAKING TO YOU?

_____

_____

_____

_____

_____

_____

_____

_____

_____

_____

_____

Be anxious for nothing, but in everything, by prayer and supplication with gratitude, make your requests known to God. And the peace of God, which surpasses all understanding, will protect your hearts and minds through Christ Jesus.

—PHILIPPIANS 4:6–7

_____

_____

_____

_____

_____

_____

_____

_____

_____

BATTLE PLANS AND BREAKTHROUGHS

WHAT IS THE LORD SPEAKING TO YOU?

_____

_____

_____

_____

_____

_____

_____

_____

_____

_____

Truly I say to you, whatever you bind on
earth will be bound in heaven, and whatever
you loose on earth will be loosed in heaven.
Again I say to you, that if two of you agree on
earth about anything they ask, it will be done
for them by My Father who is in heaven.

—MATTHEW 18:18–19

_____

_____

_____

_____

_____

_____

_____

_____

_____

BATTLE PLANS AND BREAKTHROUGHS

WHAT IS THE LORD SPEAKING TO YOU?

_____

_____

_____

_____

_____

_____

_____

_____

_____

_____

Be sober and watchful, because your adversary the devil walks around as a roaring lion, seeking whom he may devour.

—1 PETER 5:8

_____

_____

_____

_____

_____

_____

_____

_____

_____

Battle Plans and Breakthroughs

WHAT IS THE LORD SPEAKING TO YOU?

_____

_____

_____

_____

_____

_____

_____

_____

_____

_____

For God has not given us the spirit of fear,
but of power, and love, and self-control.

—2 TIMOTHY 1:7

_____

_____

_____

_____

_____

_____

_____

_____

_____

_____

BATTLE PLANS AND
BREAKTHROUGHS

WHAT IS THE LORD SPEAKING TO YOU?

_____

_____

_____

_____

_____

_____

_____

_____

_____

_____

I pursued my enemies and overtook them; I did not return until they were consumed. I wounded them, and they were not able to rise; they fell under my feet. For You girded me with strength for the battle; You subdued under me those who rose up against me.

—PSALM 18:37–39

_____

_____

_____

_____

_____

_____

_____

_____

_____

BATTLE PLANS AND
BREAKTHROUGHS

THE WILES OF THE DEVIL

EPHESIANS 6:11 INSTRUCTS us, "Put on the whole armor of God that you may be able to stand against the schemes of the devil." The purpose of the armor is to protect us and empower us as we stand against the *wiles*—the trickery, the deception, and the schemes—of the devil. His subtle tactics can take various forms, including the following.

Deception and lies: The devil is the father of lies (John 8:44) and takes the truth and twists it, mixing lies with what's good and godly. He's a master at making wrong seem right, but we can't fall for his tricks!

Temptation: The devil knows our weaknesses, and he'll use them against us. He'll dangle all sorts of temptations in front of us, promising pleasure and success.

Spiritual attacks and oppression: The devil will tear us down, rob us of our peace, and destroy our faith, so he creates obstacles and roadblocks that keep us from fulfilling our purpose. He weighs us down with burdens, feelings of despair, and hopelessness and tells us lies straight from the pit of hell.

Distraction and worldly allure: The devil knows if he can get our eyes off the things of God, he can lead us astray. So he fills our lives with noise and busyness, causing us to lose our focus and tempting us to prioritize the things of this world over our walk with the Lord.

Division and discord: The devil wants nothing more than to see us divided, so he focuses us on our differences rather than our shared values and beliefs. By fueling conflicts, fostering bitterness, and promoting a spirit of division, he attempts to weaken the unity and effectiveness of the church.

Counterfeit spirituality: The devil presents false spiritual experiences, counterfeit miracles, and deceptive signs and wonders to mislead and deceive "even the elect" (Mark 13:22). He will try to throw us off course, lead us astray with his smoke and mirrors, and get us chasing after signs and wonders instead of standing firm on the solid rock of God's Word.

Recognizing the wiles of the devil requires spiritual discernment rooted in a deep understanding of God's Word and a close relationship with Him. If you put on the whole armor of God to stand righteously, you will not fall prey to the devil's wiles, and you'll be equipped to stand through every attack, no matter how threatening or dangerous.

—GREG LOCKE, *WEAPONS OF OUR WARFARE*

DATE:

WHAT IS THE LORD SPEAKING TO YOU?

_____

_____

_____

_____

_____

_____

_____

_____

_____

_____

And above all, taking the shield of faith,
with which you will be able to extin-
guish all the fiery arrows of the evil one.

—EPHESIANS 6:16

_____

_____

_____

_____

_____

_____

_____

_____

_____

_____

BATTLE PLANS AND BREAKTHROUGHS

WHAT IS THE LORD SPEAKING TO YOU?

_____

_____

_____

_____

_____

_____

_____

_____

_____

_____

_____

> How God anointed Jesus of Nazareth with
> the Holy Spirit and with power, who went
> about doing good and healing all who were
> oppressed by the devil, for God was with Him.
>
> —ACTS 10:38

_____

_____

_____

_____

_____

_____

_____

_____

_____

BATTLE PLANS AND
BREAKTHROUGHS

WHAT IS THE LORD SPEAKING TO YOU?

_____

_____

_____

_____

_____

_____

_____

_____

_____

_____

_____

These signs will accompany those who
believe: In My name they will cast out
demons; they will speak with new tongues.

—MARK 16:17

_____

_____

_____

_____

_____

_____

_____

_____

_____

_____

BATTLE PLANS AND
BREAKTHROUGHS

WHAT IS THE LORD SPEAKING TO YOU?

_____

_____

_____

_____

_____

_____

_____

_____

_____

_____

> But the anointing which you have received
> from Him remains in you, and you do
> not need anyone to teach you. For as the
> same anointing teaches you concerning
> all things, and is truth, and is no lie, and
> just as it has taught you, remain in Him.
>
> —1 JOHN 2:27

56

_____

_____

_____

_____

_____

_____

_____

_____

_____

BATTLE PLANS AND
BREAKTHROUGHS

WHAT IS THE LORD SPEAKING TO YOU?

_____

_____

_____

_____

_____

_____

_____

_____

_____

_____

Or else how can one enter a strong man's house
and plunder his goods unless he first binds the
strong man? And then he will plunder his house.

—MATTHEW 12:29

_____

_____

_____

_____

_____

_____

_____

_____

_____

_____

BATTLE PLANS AND
BREAKTHROUGHS

WHAT IS THE LORD SPEAKING TO YOU?

_____

_____

_____

_____

_____

_____

_____

_____

_____

_____

The LORD is my rock and my fortress and
my deliverer; my God, my rock, in whom I
take refuge; my shield and the horn of my
salvation, my stronghold. I will call upon
the LORD, who is worthy to be praised, so
shall I be saved from my enemies.

—PSALM 18:2–3

_____

_____

_____

_____

_____

_____

_____

_____

_____

BATTLE PLANS AND BREAKTHROUGHS

DATE:

WHAT IS THE LORD SPEAKING TO YOU?

_____

_____

_____

_____

_____

_____

_____

_____

_____

_____

> The cords of death encompassed me, and the
> pangs of Sheol took hold of me; I found trouble
> and sorrow. Then I called upon the name of
> the LORD: "O LORD, I beseech You, deliver my
> soul." Gracious is the LORD, and righteous; yes,
> our God is merciful. The LORD preserves the
> simple; I was brought low, and He saved me.
>
> —PSALM 116:3–6

_____

_____

_____

_____

_____

_____

_____

_____

_____

_____

BATTLE PLANS AND
BREAKTHROUGHS

DATE:

WHAT IS THE LORD SPEAKING TO YOU?

_____

_____

_____

_____

_____

_____

_____

_____

_____

_____

_____

But let all those who take refuge in
You rejoice; let them ever shout for joy,
because You defend them; let those who
love Your name be joyful in You.

—PSALM 5:11

_____

_____

_____

_____

_____

_____

_____

_____

_____

_____

Battle Plans and Breakthroughs

WHAT IS THE LORD SPEAKING TO YOU?

> He called His twelve disciples to Him and gave them authority over unclean spirits, to cast them out, and to heal all kinds of sickness and all kinds of disease...."As you go, preach, saying, 'The kingdom of heaven is at hand.' Heal the sick, cleanse the lepers, raise the dead, and cast out demons. Freely you have received, freely give."
>
> —MATTHEW 10:1, 7–8

_____

_____

_____

_____

_____

_____

_____

_____

_____

_____

BATTLE PLANS AND BREAKTHROUGHS

WHAT IS THE LORD SPEAKING TO YOU?

_____

_____

_____

_____

_____

_____

_____

_____

_____

_____

Proclaim this among the nations: Consecrate a
war! Stir up the mighty men! Let all the men
of war draw near and rise. Beat your plough-
shares into swords and your pruning hooks into
spears; let the weakling say, "I am a warrior!"

—JOEL 3:9–10

_____

_____

_____

_____

_____

_____

_____

_____

_____

BATTLE PLANS AND BREAKTHROUGHS

WHAT IS THE LORD SPEAKING TO YOU?

_____

_____

_____

_____

_____

_____

_____

_____

_____

_____

_____

And [You] have not delivered me into
the hand of the enemy; You have
set my feet in a broad place.

—PSALM 31:8

_____

_____

_____

_____

_____

_____

_____

_____

_____

BATTLE PLANS AND
BREAKTHROUGHS

EIGHT SIGNS YOU MIGHT HAVE A DEMON

UNDERSTANDING HOW DEMONS operate can help us identify whether they might be hiding in our lives. Not everything is a demon; some things are the flesh. But there are key signs of demonic activity to watch for. Let's discuss eight signs you might have a demon hiding.

1. Manifesting a demon

If you manifest a demon, meaning a demon surfaces, you know right away a demon is there, and you can now deal with it. Some manifestations might include a demon starting to laugh out of the person being delivered, demons speaking out, saying, "How did you know I am here?," demons making the person slither like a snake or do abnormal body contortions, hysterical laughing or crying, growling or making animal noises, a racing heartbeat, sweating profusely when talking about deliverance or receiving deliverance prayer, feeling extremely nervous when talking about deliverance—the list is long, but these are some main manifestations. In all honesty, I would not consider manifesting a sign that a demon *might* be hiding, because if you manifest, the demon is no longer hiding. It is out in the open.

2. Dominating/intrusive thoughts

These are thoughts you did not create, the Holy Spirit did not give you, and that are extremely hard to get rid of. They also usually come at unconventional times and without reason. I've had the most normal people you can imagine say, "I had a random thought that I should kill my wife [or my kid]. I would never in a million years do that, but this thought was so overwhelming!"

In 2010 before I was delivered, I remember sitting down to eat breakfast one day and getting the most twisted and perverted thoughts. I knew it wasn't me but didn't know what it was. I know now it was a demon, but sadly, at the time, I thought it was just normal. In early 2011 I was delivered, and to this day I've never had thoughts like that. Likely, you know exactly what

I mean when I say these thoughts are dominating. They feel as though they suffocate you and don't let you up for air.

3. Voices in your head

This is a dead giveaway. If you have a voice speaking to you, saying things like "us," "we," "Let's go do this," "We should say this," and so forth, that is a demon talking to you. If a voice says, "I am going to do this to you," that is a demon talking. A girl I recently interviewed on my podcast who shared her deliverance story told me every time she would walk into a room with people in it, voices in her head would say, "They hate you. Nobody here likes you. Nobody wants you here. You're ugly," and so on. These voices would say all kinds of foul things to her and about her. She convinced herself it was her own thoughts, but after going through deliverance, she realized those were demons talking to her the entire time.

Only two voices can speak to our minds: the Holy Spirit's and demons'. It's obvious that the Holy Spirit would never say those things, so we can easily conclude that they were demons.

4. Hatred toward others for no apparent reason

If you're experiencing hatred toward a specific race, parents, friends, church leaders, authority figures such as police officers, and so forth, this is likely demonic. Before I went through deliverance, I was racist toward my *own* race! How twisted is that, to be racist against yourself, yet that is exactly how demons manipulated and deceived me. Demons love to breed hatred into the hearts of humans to try to divide and conquer us. (See Matthew 12:25–26.)

The purpose of the devil making you hate your fellow brother is to cause division. It amazes me how many Christians hate deliverance ministers for no reason. Well, there is a reason: The demons are causing them to hate ministries that destroy Satan's kingdom. The theme I hope you're picking up is "without reason."

5. Physical symptoms that have no medical reasoning

Demons are often the cause of sickness and disease, and one of the dead giveaways of sickness being caused by a demon is when doctors have no explanation for it. Many people come to me and say, "I have a specific pain in my body, and I've been to every doctor, and everything checks out. I'm healthy." This is a telltale sign that a demon may be causing that specific sickness or pain. Luke 13:10–13 is a perfect example of this. It tells of a woman who was severely crippled, not from a natural sickness that doctors could diagnose but from a demonic "spirit of infirmity" (v. 10). Jesus did not say to go see a doctor. Jesus loosed her from her infirmity, and immediately her back was straight. What doctors couldn't do in a lifetime, Jesus did in a moment!

I had a good friend whose little sister was extremely sick all the time, and doctors could not help her. One day we went to her house to pray for her, and the Holy Spirit told me she didn't need healing. She needed deliverance. Sure enough, as we began to pray and command the spirit of infirmity out of her, there was a dramatic manifestation and then freedom. After this deliverance she never had those symptoms of sickness again.

It is so vital we listen to the Holy Spirit, because sometimes we try to pray for healing when really we should be praying for deliverance. Often in the New Testament you will see that when Jesus prayed for the sick, He also cast out demons. (See Matthew 8:16–17, for example.) So it's not one or the other; it's both!

6. Recurring nightmares/night terrors
Demons love to attack at night—it is when we are most vulnerable to spiritual attack. Although our bodies are asleep, our spirits do not sleep, and demons take advantage of this fact. You might wake up feeling a weight on your chest, not be able to speak the name of Jesus, see a dark figure at the foot of your bed or corner of your room, or have the feeling of being suffocated. People who are demonized seem to be much more prone to being attacked by demons in their sleep.

If someone is having nonstop nightmares, I always recommend they seek out deliverance. A helpful tip is to pray for the armor of God before bed. I make it a nightly thing before bed to pray the full armor of God. It is very important you be careful what you watch before bed, as watching horror movies, crime documentaries, and shows like that makes you extremely susceptible to demonic attack. Here is a scripture I like to quote before bed if I am dealing with attacks at night: "You shall not be afraid of the terror by night, nor of the arrow that flies by day" (Ps. 91:5). The same God who protects you in the day will also protect you at night.

7. Mental illnesses

This is a very controversial one, and let me be the first to say I do not believe every mental illness is demonic, but I believe some are. Put it this way: If you go to a doctor and say, "I hear voices," or, "I have multiple personalities," they're not going to say, "You have a demon. Go get deliverance." They are likely going to diagnose you with a mental illness and put you on medication.

According to the National Institute of Mental Health, hearing voices is a main symptom of schizophrenia. Yet we know that it is also a main symptom of demonization. Do you see how these two things cross paths? If you begin to look into many mental illnesses today, you will see demons are responsible for not all but some of them. You might say, "Well, Isaiah, I have a mental illness, but it's not a demon. Is there hope for me?" Yes, because we serve a God who heals and delivers! I rest my point. The rabbit hole on this goes deep; just know that oftentimes mental illness is a sign of a demon.

8. Irrational fears and phobias

This is a major sign that a demon is hiding, especially when you have fears that are irrational in nature. I've dealt with people who are deathly afraid of harmless animals. One woman we did deliverance on was terrified of birds. She had no clue why she was like this, but during her deliverance an ancient bird spirit manifested to the point she was making bird noises. This might sound crazy to you, but for her it was very real. After her deliverance, that phobia of birds completely left her. If you or someone you know is dealing with an irrational fear or phobia, it's likely from a demon.

There are many different signs you may have a demon hiding, but these are the most common, in my opinion.

—ISAIAH SALDIVAR, *HOW TO CAST OUT DEMONS*

WHAT IS THE LORD SPEAKING TO YOU?

_____

_____

_____

_____

_____

_____

_____

_____

_____

_____

I am the vine, you are the branches. He who remains in Me, and I in him, bears much fruit. For without Me you can do nothing.

—JOHN 15:5

_____

_____

_____

_____

_____

_____

_____

_____

_____

Battle Plans and Breakthroughs

DATE:

WHAT IS THE LORD SPEAKING TO YOU?

_____

_____

_____

_____

_____

_____

_____

_____

_____

_____

> By this I know that You are well
> pleased with me: because my enemy
> does not triumph over me.
>
> —PSALM 41:11

_____

_____

_____

_____

_____

_____

_____

_____

_____

BATTLE PLANS AND BREAKTHROUGHS

WHAT IS THE LORD SPEAKING TO YOU?

_____

_____

_____

_____

_____

_____

_____

_____

_____

_____

_____

Let your lives be without love of money, and be
content with the things you have. For He has
said: "I will never leave you, nor forsake you."

—HEBREWS 13:5

_____

_____

_____

_____

_____

_____

_____

_____

_____

BATTLE PLANS AND
BREAKTHROUGHS

WHAT IS THE LORD SPEAKING TO YOU?

_____

_____

_____

_____

_____

_____

_____

_____

_____

_____

For You have been my refuge, a
strong tower against the enemy.

—PSALM 61:3

_____

_____

_____

_____

_____

_____

_____

_____

_____

BATTLE PLANS AND BREAKTHROUGHS

DATE:

WHAT IS THE LORD SPEAKING TO YOU?

_____

_____

_____

_____

_____

_____

_____

_____

_____

_____

This is the confidence that we have in
Him, that if we ask anything according to
His will, He hears us. So if we know that
He hears whatever we ask, we know that
we have whatever we asked of Him.

—1 JOHN 5:14–15

_____

_____

_____

_____

_____

_____

_____

_____

_____

BATTLE PLANS AND BREAKTHROUGHS

DATE:

WHAT IS THE LORD SPEAKING TO YOU?

_____

_____

_____

_____

_____

_____

_____

_____

_____

_____

Give ear, O LORD, to my prayer; and
attend to the voice of my supplica-
tions. In the day of my trouble I will call
upon You, for You will answer me.

—PSALM 86:6–7

86

_____

_____

_____

_____

_____

_____

_____

_____

_____

BATTLE PLANS AND
BREAKTHROUGHS

WHAT IS THE LORD SPEAKING TO YOU?

_____

_____

_____

_____

_____

_____

_____

_____

_____

_____

_____

You will keep him in perfect peace, whose mind
is stayed on You, because he trusts in You.

—Isaiah 26:3

_____

_____

_____

_____

_____

_____

_____

_____

_____

BATTLE PLANS AND BREAKTHROUGHS

WHAT IS THE LORD SPEAKING TO YOU?

_____

_____

_____

_____

_____

_____

_____

_____

_____

_____

Let the redeemed of the LORD say so, whom He
has redeemed from the hand of the enemy, and
gathered from the lands, from the east and from
the west, from the north and from the south.

—PSALM 107:2–3

_____

_____

_____

_____

_____

_____

_____

_____

_____

_____

Battle Plans and Breakthroughs

WHAT IS THE LORD SPEAKING TO YOU?

_____

_____

_____

_____

_____

_____

_____

_____

_____

_____

No, in all these things we are more than
conquerors through Him who loved us.

—ROMANS 8:37

_____

_____

_____

_____

_____

_____

_____

_____

_____

BATTLE PLANS AND
BREAKTHROUGHS

WHAT IS THE LORD SPEAKING TO YOU?

_____

_____

_____

_____

_____

_____

_____

_____

_____

_____

He has delivered us from the power
of darkness and has transferred us
into the kingdom of His dear Son.

—COLOSSIANS 1:13

_____

_____

_____

_____

_____

_____

_____

_____

_____

BATTLE PLANS AND
BREAKTHROUGHS

WHAT IS THE LORD SPEAKING TO YOU?

_____

_____

_____

_____

_____

_____

_____

_____

_____

_____

Who are protected by the power of
God through faith for a salvation ready
to be revealed in the last time.

—1 PETER 1:5

_____

_____

_____

_____

_____

_____

_____

_____

_____

_____

BATTLE PLANS AND BREAKTHROUGHS

WATCH IN PRAYER

EVERY FOOT SOLDIER at one time or another is assigned to patrol duty. They are assigned to *take a watch* at the front gates or in one of the towers surrounding the camp. They do this to keep out intruders, warn those within if there is an attack, or inform their commanders of approaching messengers. They also do it as an exercise in vigilance, even if it doesn't seem like there is anything to be watchful for. Setting out a watch is one of the most basic of defensive tactics. No matter how strong your walls, if a watch is not set, the enemy will find a way in.

In the days during which the Old Testament was still being written cities would set watchmen on the walls for these same purposes. These watchers had to be vigilant, stay awake, and endure the elements no matter the conditions. These watches were often long, boring, and uneventful, but they were still necessary. The reason for this is obvious: If the watchmen failed, the city would fall.

For those in the cities of Israel the watchmen also had another duty: to pray. As God told Israel through Isaiah, "I have set watchmen on your walls, O Jerusalem, who shall never hold their peace day or night. You who remind the LORD, do not keep silent; give Him no rest until He establishes and makes Jerusalem a glory in the earth" (Isa. 62:6–7).

Just as watching in prayer was the first line of defense between the people of Israel and any peoples that might seek their harm, so watching and praying are the essential defensive disciplines for every believer. In fact, Jesus said they would be our primary responsibilities until He returns to the earth.

> Take heed, watch and pray. For you do not know when the time [of My return] will come. For the Son of Man is like a man leaving on a far journey who left his house and gave authority to his servants and to every man his work, and commanded the porter to watch. Watch therefore—for you do not know when the master of the house is coming, in the evening, or at midnight, or at

cockcrow, or in the morning—lest he come suddenly and find you sleeping. What I say to you I say to all: Watch!
—MARK 13:33–37

If the church has failed, it is because our watchmen have failed. If our spiritual hedges of protection have been breached, it is because they were weakened through negligence. The evangelical movement that was birthed in fervent prayer is reeling today because we have gone from telling people they must pray through until they know they are saved to dishing out a prescribed prayer when they come forward in response to an altar call. Our watchmen and women have grown slack in their duties because they have been trained in complacency. We don't see miracles as they did in the old days simply because we don't value prayer as they did. We must purposefully set and revitalize our watches.

In ancient Israel watches were set out in three-hour shifts, beginning at sundown (6:00 p.m.) and then circling the clock after that (thus the watches changed at 9:00 p.m., 12:00 a.m., 3:00 a.m., 6:00 a.m., 9:00 a.m., 12:00 p.m., 3:00 p.m., and then again at 6:00 p.m.). Each of these watches had its own prayer assignment and area of strategic intercession. With the information that follows, each of these biblical watches can become a significant prayer watch for the believer today.

6:00 p.m.–9:00 p.m.—Evening/Transformational Watch

Prayer focus: This is a time of supplication, confession, repentance, and strategic and prophetic national and global intercession. Ask God to slay the evening wolves according to Habakkuk 1.

Important scriptures: Genesis 1:5; Daniel 9:1–23; 10:1–14. God works from evening to morning.

> I will stand at my watch and station myself on the watchtower; and I will keep watch to see what He will say to me, and what I will answer when I am reproved.
> —HABAKKUK 2:1

9:00 p.m.–12:00 a.m.—Night/Seeking Watch

Prayer focus: This is the time when tremendous revelation begins to flow. Like Daniel, do not leave the presence of God until He has fully downloaded the complete revelation He has for you.

Important scriptures: Song of Solomon 3:1–4; Jeremiah 6:5; Acts 20:7

12:00 a.m.–3:00 a.m.—Transitional/Breakthrough Watch

Prayer focus: This is the demonic/bewitching hour when there are high demonic activities. Pray that the strongman be bound. You must deal the enemy a death blow. In the world this is the beginning of the graveyard shift. Declare that the plots and plans of the enemy will be overthrown.

Important scriptures: Exodus 11:4; 12:29; Judges 16:3; Ruth 3:8; 1 Kings 3:20; Job 34:20; Acts 16:25

3:00 a.m.–6:00 a.m.—Graveyard/Prophetic Watch

Prayer focus: Be careful of the demonic ambush of sleepiness. You must continue to wrestle until you see the face of God.

Important scriptures: Genesis 32:24–30; Matthew 26:34

6:00 a.m.–9:00 a.m.—Breakthrough Watch

Prayer focus: This is the breaking of a new day/cycle watch. Pray that God will make all things new for fresh starts. Prepare yourself to receive new and fresh revelation. Continue to declare victory over all your adverse situations and circumstances.

Important scriptures: Numbers 2:1–3; Isaiah 59:16–21; Malachi 1:11; Mark 16:2

9:00 a.m.–12:00 p.m.—Morning Watch

Prayer focus: This hour is dedicated to breaking up the fallow ground, plowing, and planting. Use God's Word in prayer. Spend time reading Scripture and in praise and worship. Expect strong prophetic winds to blow. You will receive visions and angelic visitation as well.

Important scriptures: Nehemiah 8:1–3; Matthew 20:5–6; Acts 10:1–4. Pray according to Exodus 14:24–31 and Psalm 68:1–4.

12:00 p.m.–3:00 p.m.—Transitional/Apostolic Supernatural Watch

Prayer focus: This is a time for strong spiritual warfare, also a time for corporate gathering of the saints for supernatural deliverance and miracles. War and protect your prophetic destiny and those things that God has manifested as blessings. Once you have prophetically birthed something, you must build prayer shields and fire walls to protect it from premature death.

Important scriptures: 1 Kings 18:19–40; 20; 2 Kings 4:20; Jeremiah 6:4; Zephaniah 2:1–4; Matthew 26:45–54; Acts 22:6

3:00 p.m.–6:00 p.m.—Afternoon Watch

Prayer focus: As the sun sets, press in to the secret place of God for protection. This is a time for heavy seduction to give in to temptation for your entire church body. While most people are out and about, you will be tempted to follow likewise. Ask God to protect your resources, ministerial staff, helps ministers, support staff, business relationships, employees, and others from the spirit of Belial. This is an hour that is not strongly covered. The enemy knows when we are uncovered, and he strikes at this time.

Important scriptures: Judges 19:1–30

—CINDY TRIMM, *THE ART OF WAR FOR SPIRITUAL BATTLE*

WHAT IS THE LORD SPEAKING TO YOU?

_____

_____

_____

_____

_____

_____

_____

_____

_____

_____

In whom we have boldness and confident access through faith in Him.

—EPHESIANS 3:12

_____

_____

_____

_____

_____

_____

_____

_____

_____

_____

Battle Plans and
Breakthroughs

WHAT IS THE LORD SPEAKING TO YOU?

For thus says the Lord GOD, the Holy One
of Israel: In returning and rest you shall be
saved; in quietness and in confidence shall
be your strength. Yet you were not willing.

—ISAIAH 30:15

_____

_____

_____

_____

_____

_____

_____

_____

_____

_____

BATTLE PLANS AND
BREAKTHROUGHS

WHAT IS THE LORD SPEAKING TO YOU?

_____

_____

_____

_____

_____

_____

_____

_____

_____

_____

_____

> To You will I cry, O LORD my rock; do not
> be silent to me, lest, if You are silent to
> me, I become like those who go down
> to the pit. Hear the voice of my supplica-
> tions when I cry to You, when I lift up my
> hands toward Your most holy place.
>
> —PSALM 28:1–2

_____

_____

_____

_____

_____

_____

_____

_____

_____

_____

Battle Plans and Breakthroughs

DATE:

WHAT IS THE LORD SPEAKING TO YOU?

_____

_____

_____

_____

_____

_____

_____

_____

_____

_____

_____

For the LORD will be your confidence and
will keep your foot from being caught.

—PROVERBS 3:26

_____

_____

_____

_____

_____

_____

_____

_____

_____

_____

BATTLE PLANS AND
BREAKTHROUGHS

DATE:

WHAT IS THE LORD SPEAKING TO YOU?

_____

_____

_____

_____

_____

_____

_____

_____

_____

_____

> And he sought after God in the days of
> Zechariah, the one who instructed him in the
> fear of the LORD. And in the days that he sought
> after the LORD, God caused him to succeed.
>
> —2 CHRONICLES 26:5

_____

_____

_____

_____

_____

_____

_____

_____

_____

BATTLE PLANS AND
BREAKTHROUGHS

DATE:

WHAT IS THE LORD SPEAKING TO YOU?

_____

_____

_____

_____

_____

_____

_____

_____

_____

_____

_____

> You who fear the LORD, trust in the LORD!
> He is their help and their shield.
>
> —PSALM 115:11

112

_____

_____

_____

_____

_____

_____

_____

_____

_____

BATTLE PLANS AND
BREAKTHROUGHS

DATE:

WHAT IS THE LORD SPEAKING TO YOU?

_____

_____

_____

_____

_____

_____

_____

_____

_____

_____

> Blessed be the God and Father of our
> Lord Jesus Christ, who has blessed us
> with every spiritual blessing in the heav-
> enly places in Christ, just as He chose us in
> Him before the foundation of the world, to
> be holy and blameless before Him in love.
>
> —EPHESIANS 1:3–4

_____

_____

_____

_____

_____

_____

_____

_____

_____

_____

BATTLE PLANS AND
BREAKTHROUGHS

WHAT IS THE LORD SPEAKING TO YOU?

_____

_____

_____

_____

_____

_____

_____

_____

_____

_____

_____

Though he fall, he shall not be utterly cast
down, for the LORD upholds him with His hand.

—PSALM 37:24

_____

_____

_____

_____

_____

_____

_____

_____

_____

BATTLE PLANS AND BREAKTHROUGHS

WHAT IS THE LORD SPEAKING TO YOU?

_____

_____

_____

_____

_____

_____

_____

_____

_____

_____

_____

Now thanks be to God who always causes us
to triumph in Christ and through us reveals the
fragrance of His knowledge in every place.

—2 CORINTHIANS 2:14

_____

_____

_____

_____

_____

_____

_____

_____

_____

BATTLE PLANS AND BREAKTHROUGHS

WHAT IS THE LORD SPEAKING TO YOU?

_____

_____

_____

_____

_____

_____

_____

_____

_____

_____

All Scripture is inspired by God and is prof-
itable for teaching, for reproof, for correc-
tion, and for training in righteousness, that
the man of God may be complete, thor-
oughly equipped for every good work.

—2 TIMOTHY 3:16–17

BATTLE PLANS AND BREAKTHROUGHS

DATE:

WHAT IS THE LORD SPEAKING TO YOU?

_____

_____

_____

_____

_____

_____

_____

_____

_____

_____

_____

Many are the afflictions of the righteous, but
the LORD delivers him out of them all.

—PSALM 34:19

_____

_____

_____

_____

_____

_____

_____

_____

_____

_____

BATTLE PLANS AND BREAKTHROUGHS

FASTING FOR BREAKTHROUGH

THERE ARE DIFFERENT kinds of demons. Some are easy to cast out of your life; others just don't give up. They are arrogant and defiant. And you may have to do something unusual, extraordinary, and beyond the norm to see breakthrough. Some sweet little prayer is not going to do it. It is going to take an anointing that destroys the yoke. When you fast, the anointing increases in your life. The authority, power, and faith of God come alive when you lay aside some things and fast. You will find yourself getting stronger and stronger.

Isaiah 58 talks about how we can fast to break every yoke and undo the heavy burdens. Fasting makes room so the oppressed go free. Fasting breaks bondages and causes revival. When you are dealing with a serious issue that perhaps you don't know how to handle, sometimes the best thing to do is let go of some food for a little while and pray against that thing.

As you humble yourself through fasting, the grace of God will come upon your life. The Lord will be the strength of your life. What you could not do in the flesh you will be able to do by the Spirit of God. It's not by might nor by power but by the Spirit of the Lord that every mountain is removed!

Fasting has many benefits, but one is that it can release the breaker anointing. Micah prophesied that the day of the breaker was coming up before his people. We are living in that day.

> He who breaks through has gone up before them; they will break through and pass the gate and go out by it. Then their king will pass on before them, the LORD at their head.
>
> —MICAH 2:13

The Lord is a breaker. He is able to break through any obstacle or opposition on behalf of His covenant people. Fasting will cause breakthroughs to continue in families, cities, nations, finances, and churches. It will help believers break through all opposition from the enemy. A life of consistent fasting will cause many victories to manifest. God's will is that His covenant believers live lives of victory and perfect peace, with nothing being impossible to them.

FAST IN THE RIGHT SPIRIT

In Jesus' day the Pharisees fasted with attitudes of pride and superiority.

> The Pharisee stood and prayed these things about himself, "God, I thank You that I am not like other men....I fast twice a week."
>
> —LUKE 18:11–12

Anytime you are full of pride, being legalistic and religious, you can fast and pray all you want, but you won't see many miracles. The Pharisees didn't experience any miracles as a result of their prayer and fasting. They had no power. They couldn't heal a hangnail. The Pharisees had nothing but long robes—robes with no miracles. Jesus performed many miracles because He was humble and full of mercy, love, and compassion toward people.

We must approach fasting with humility. Fasting must be genuine and not religious or hypocritical. This is what God requires in fasting. We must have correct motives in fasting. Fasting is a powerful tool if done correctly. Muslims and Hindus fast, but their fasts are merely religious. Great miracles and breakthroughs happen when fasting is done in the right spirit.

Isaiah chapter 58 describes the fast that God has chosen:

- Fasting cannot be done with amusement (v. 3).

- Fasting cannot be done while mistreating others (v. 3).

- Fasting cannot be done for strife or contention (v. 4).

- Fasting should cause one to bow his head in humility, as a bulrush (v. 5).

- Fasting should be a time of searching the heart and repenting.

- Fasting should be done with an attitude of compassion for the lost and hurting (v. 7).

This is the fast that God promises to bless.

The enemy knows the power of prayer and fasting, and he will do everything in his power to stop you. Believers who begin to fast can expect to encounter much spiritual resistance. A believer must be committed to a fasted lifestyle. The rewards of fasting far outweigh the obstacles of the enemy.

WAYS TO FAST

Fasting is beneficial whether you fast partially or fully. Practicing one-day fasts on a consistent basis will strengthen your spirit over time and give you the ability to discipline yourself for longer fasts. Three-day fasts with just water are a powerful way to see breakthroughs. Fasts longer than three days should be done by people with more experience in fasting.

I do not recommend long fasts unless there is an emergency or one is led by the Holy Spirit to do so. Daniel fasted twenty-one days and saw a great breakthrough for his people (Dan. 9–10). Daniel was also a prophet, and God will use prophets who fast for different reasons to bring breakthroughs. Jesus fasted for forty days before beginning His ministry. I do know of people who have fasted forty days and have seen great breakthroughs.

A partial fast can include eating some food such as vegetables and can be done for a long period of time. Complete fasts consist of only water, and water is important to cleanse the system of toxins that are released through fasting. The Holy Spirit will reveal to you when you need to fast.

FASTING RELEASES BREAKTHROUGH

Fasting coupled with prayer is one of the most powerful weapons you can use to release breakthrough. As a covenant believer deliverance and freedom are part of your salvation package. The enemy fights you for this freedom. This is why we are in a battle.

When you begin to fast and pray for the enemy's hands to be taken off your stuff, the following is what you can expect to be released.

- Fasting will release God's glory for your protection (Isa. 58:8).

- Fasting will result in answered prayer (Isa. 58:9).

- Fasting releases divine guidance (Isa. 58:11).

- Fasting will cause you to have great victory against overwhelming odds (2 Chron. 20:2–3).

- Fasting will release the power of the Holy Spirit for the miraculous to occur (Luke 4:14, 18).

A fasted lifestyle is a powerful lifestyle. When you are challenged with unbelief in a situation or are facing a stubborn demon, I encourage you to fast and pray for breakthrough.

—JOHN ECKHARDT, *DELIVERANCE AND SPIRITUAL WARFARE MANUAL*

WHAT IS THE LORD SPEAKING TO YOU?

_____

_____

_____

_____

_____

_____

_____

_____

_____

Then your light shall break forth as the morning,
and your healing shall spring forth quickly, and
your righteousness shall go before you; the
glory of the LORD shall be your rear guard.

—ISAIAH 58:8

_____

_____

_____

_____

_____

_____

_____

_____

_____

BATTLE PLANS AND BREAKTHROUGHS

WHAT IS THE LORD SPEAKING TO YOU?

_____

_____

_____

_____

_____

_____

_____

_____

_____

_____

_____

Yet a little while, and the wicked will
be no more; though you look diligently
for his place, he will not be there.

—PSALM 37:10

_____

_____

_____

_____

_____

_____

_____

_____

_____

_____

BATTLE PLANS AND BREAKTHROUGHS

WHAT IS THE LORD SPEAKING TO YOU?

_____

_____

_____

_____

_____

_____

_____

_____

_____

_____

> The Spirit of the Lord GOD is upon me
> because the LORD has anointed me to preach
> good news to the poor; He has sent me to
> heal the broken-hearted, to proclaim lib-
> erty to the captives, and the opening of
> the prison to those who are bound.
>
> —ISAIAH 61:1

_____

_____

_____

_____

_____

_____

_____

_____

_____

BATTLE PLANS AND BREAKTHROUGHS

DATE:

WHAT IS THE LORD SPEAKING TO YOU?

_____

_____

_____

_____

_____

_____

_____

_____

_____

_____

The wicked plots against the righteous, and
gnashes his teeth at him. The Lord laughs
at him, for He sees that his day is coming.

—PSALM 37:12–13

_____

_____

_____

_____

_____

_____

_____

_____

_____

Battle Plans and Breakthroughs

DATE:

WHAT IS THE LORD SPEAKING TO YOU?

_____

_____

_____

_____

_____

_____

_____

_____

_____

_____

The LORD is good, a stronghold in
the day of distress; and He knows
those who take refuge in Him.

—NAHUM 1:7

136

_____

_____

_____

_____

_____

_____

_____

_____

_____

BATTLE PLANS AND BREAKTHROUGHS

WHAT IS THE LORD SPEAKING TO YOU?

_____

_____

_____

_____

_____

_____

_____

_____

_____

_____

Therefore if the Son sets you free,
you shall be free indeed.

—JOHN 8:36

_____

_____

_____

_____

_____

_____

_____

_____

_____

BATTLE PLANS AND BREAKTHROUGHS

WHAT IS THE LORD SPEAKING TO YOU?

_____

_____

_____

_____

_____

_____

_____

_____

_____

_____

Do not rejoice over me, my enemy! Although
I have fallen, I will rise; although I dwell
in darkness, the LORD is my light.

—MICAH 7:8

_____

_____

_____

_____

_____

_____

_____

_____

_____

_____

BATTLE PLANS AND BREAKTHROUGHS

WHAT IS THE LORD SPEAKING TO YOU?

_____

_____

_____

_____

_____

_____

_____

_____

_____

_____

_____

For I consider that the sufferings of this
present time are not worthy to be compared
with the glory which shall be revealed to us.

—ROMANS 8:18

_____

_____

_____

_____

_____

_____

_____

_____

_____

Battle Plans and Breakthroughs

DATE:

WHAT IS THE LORD SPEAKING TO YOU?

_____

_____

_____

_____

_____

_____

_____

_____

_____

_____

_____

> Stand fast therefore in the liberty by which
> Christ has set us free, and be not entan-
> gled again with a yoke of bondage.
>
> —GALATIANS 5:1

_____

_____

_____

_____

_____

_____

_____

_____

_____

_____

BATTLE PLANS AND BREAKTHROUGHS

WHAT IS THE LORD SPEAKING TO YOU?

Who are you, O great mountain? Before
Zerubbabel you will be made level ground,
and he will bring out the top stone amidst
shouting of "Grace! Grace to the stone!"

—ZECHARIAH 4:7

_____

_____

_____

_____

_____

_____

_____

_____

_____

BATTLE PLANS AND BREAKTHROUGHS

WHAT IS THE LORD SPEAKING TO YOU?

_____

_____

_____

_____

_____

_____

_____

_____

_____

_____

_____

We know that all things work together for
good to those who love God, to those who
are called according to His purpose.

—ROMANS 8:28

_____

_____

_____

_____

_____

_____

_____

_____

_____

_____

BATTLE PLANS AND BREAKTHROUGHS

Overcoming Strongholds

IF WE WANT to defeat strongholds of the mind and experience God's peace and freedom, we must do what Paul teaches in Philippians 4:8: "Finally, brothers, whatever things are true, whatever things are honest, whatever things are just, whatever things are pure, whatever things are lovely, whatever things are of good report, if there is any virtue, and if there is any praise, think on these things." Paul is telling us that we must intentionally fix our minds on those things that reflect the truth of who God is and what He thinks about us, His dearly loved children. As we apply Paul's counsel, we will find ourselves walking victoriously in Christ. Let's look at each item in Paul's list.

Whatever things are true

Many of us focus not on things that are true, real, and honest but on things that worry us. We must remember that Satan is a liar (John 8:44). Therefore, we must determine not to accept condemning thoughts or lies from the devil, which cause us to fret about things we cannot change. Instead, we must purpose to focus on God's truth, which will empower us in our spiritual walk and in life. It is by the truth, which is the Word of God, that we are purified, consecrated, and made holy. (See John 17:17.) So if we are going to train our minds to think on what is good, we must fill ourselves with God's truth by meditating on His Word.

Whatever things are honest

We are to be people of honor, character, and dignity—and that begins with our thought life. You and I should not dwell on things that are not respectable. This does not mean we avoid or choose to be ignorant of what is unpleasant and displeasing in the world. Rather, this means we must not focus our attention on dishonorable things and permit them to control our thoughts.

Whatever things are just

A just person is one who learns to think on what God approves of and accepts. This person's way of thinking, feeling, and acting is conformed to God's will. Just individuals relate to all people from a place of kingdom love and authority. This means we always respond to people from the Father's heart of love while also speaking His truth, wisdom, and righteousness without compromise.

Whatever things are pure

As believers we are to think on what is chaste, modest, and morally pure, focusing on gracious and righteous thoughts, not on the carnal thoughts encouraged by this corrupt world.

Whatever things are lovely

In a world in which conflict is ever present, thinking on what is lovely can be an incredibly difficult task. However, we can choose to see the loveliness of God and His magnificent work in His creation. We can be the voice of truth and the example that guides others to redirect their focus to things that are lovely.

Whatever things are of good report

We can choose to be people who believe the good report and see the glass half full. We do this by learning to find what is good and positive in circumstances. Begin to discipline yourself not to linger on the negatives. Learn to think before you speak, and let the goodness of God and His report be your focus.

If there is any virtue

If something has virtue, it will motivate us to do better in every area of our lives. As Christians we cannot afford to waste mind power or emotional strength on thoughts that would tear us or others down if they were shared.

If there is any praise

If something is deserving of praise, it is worth commending to ourselves and to others. I know of no one more deserving of praise, fame, and commendation than our heavenly Father. Set your praise on Him. Choose to audibly thank Him for the things He has done for you, and praise Him in advance for the things for which you are still awaiting a spiritual breakthrough.

—REBECCA GREENWOOD, *DEFEATING STRONGHOLDS OF THE MIND*

WHAT IS THE LORD SPEAKING TO YOU?

_____

_____

_____

_____

_____

_____

_____

_____

_____

_____

The God of peace will soon crush
Satan under your feet. The grace of
our Lord Jesus Christ be with you.

—ROMANS 16:20

_____

_____

_____

_____

_____

_____

_____

_____

_____

Battle Plans and Breakthroughs

WHAT IS THE LORD SPEAKING TO YOU?

_____

_____

_____

_____

_____

_____

_____

_____

_____

_____

For You are not a God who has pleasure
in wickedness, nor will evil dwell with You.
Those who boast will not stand in Your
sight; You hate all workers of iniquity. You
will destroy those who speak lies; the LORD
abhors the bloodthirsty and deceitful man.

—PSALM 5:4–6

154

_____

_____

_____

_____

_____

_____

_____

_____

_____

BATTLE PLANS AND
BREAKTHROUGHS

WHAT IS THE LORD SPEAKING TO YOU?

_____

_____

_____

_____

_____

_____

_____

_____

_____

_____

_____

With God we shall do valiantly, for it is
He who will tread down our enemies.

—PSALM 60:12

_____

_____

_____

_____

_____

_____

_____

_____

_____

BATTLE PLANS AND BREAKTHROUGHS

DATE:

WHAT IS THE LORD SPEAKING TO YOU?

_____

_____

_____

_____

_____

_____

_____

_____

_____

_____

Call to Me, and I will answer you, and show you
great and mighty things which you do not know.

—JEREMIAH 33:3

158

_____

_____

_____

_____

_____

_____

_____

_____

_____

BATTLE PLANS AND BREAKTHROUGHS

DATE:

WHAT IS THE LORD SPEAKING TO YOU?

_____

_____

_____

_____

_____

_____

_____

_____

_____

_____

_____

> At that time I will bring you in, at the time
> when I gather you; for I will make you
> renowned and praised among all peo-
> ples of the earth, when I restore your for-
> tunes before your eyes, says the LORD.
>
> —ZEPHANIAH 3:20

_____

_____

_____

_____

_____

_____

_____

_____

_____

BATTLE PLANS AND
BREAKTHROUGHS

WHAT IS THE LORD SPEAKING TO YOU?

_____

_____

_____

_____

_____

_____

_____

_____

_____

_____

Through You we will push down our
enemies; through Your name we will
trample those who rise up against us.

—PSALM 44:5

_____

_____

_____

_____

_____

_____

_____

_____

_____

Battle Plans and Breakthroughs

WHAT IS THE LORD SPEAKING TO YOU?

_____

_____

_____

_____

_____

_____

_____

_____

_____

_____

Let God arise; let His enemies be scattered;
let those who hate Him flee before Him.

—PSALM 68:1

_____

_____

_____

_____

_____

_____

_____

_____

_____

_____

Battle Plans and Breakthroughs

WHAT IS THE LORD SPEAKING TO YOU?

_____

_____

_____

_____

_____

_____

_____

_____

_____

_____

> In righteousness you shall be established; you shall be far from oppression, for you shall not fear, and from terror, for it shall not come near you.
>
> —ISAIAH 54:14

_____

_____

_____

_____

_____

_____

_____

_____

_____

_____

BATTLE PLANS AND
BREAKTHROUGHS

WHAT IS THE LORD SPEAKING TO YOU?

_____

_____

_____

_____

_____

_____

_____

_____

_____

_____

You will hide them in the shelter of Your presence from the plots of man; You will keep them secretly in a shelter from contentious tongues.

—PSALM 31:20

_____

_____

_____

_____

_____

_____

_____

_____

_____

BATTLE PLANS AND
BREAKTHROUGHS

WHAT IS THE LORD SPEAKING TO YOU?

_____

_____

_____

_____

_____

_____

_____

_____

_____

_____

My son, let them not depart from your sight;
keep sound wisdom and discretion, and they
will be life to your soul and adornment for
your neck. Then you will walk on your way
securely, and your foot will not stumble.

—PROVERBS 3:21–23

_____

_____

_____

_____

_____

_____

_____

_____

_____

BATTLE PLANS AND BREAKTHROUGHS

WHAT IS THE LORD SPEAKING TO YOU?

For My thoughts are not your thoughts, nor
are your ways My ways, says the LORD. For
as the heavens are higher than the earth,
so are My ways higher than your ways,
and My thoughts than your thoughts.

—Isaiah 55:8–9

_____

_____

_____

_____

_____

_____

_____

_____

_____

Battle Plans and Breakthroughs

Prepare for Long War

Second Samuel 3:1 says, "Now there was a long war between the house of Saul and the house of David. But David grew stronger and stronger, and the house of Saul grew weaker and weaker" (NKJV). You may not like this term *long war*. I don't blame you. Who would? We want the battle to end quickly. But some wars don't end quickly. If you are fighting a stubborn enemy who refuses to give in to surrender, then just know it is going to fight and fight and fight. There are demons who fight and fight and fight to hold on. But I have good news for you. If you keep putting pressure on the enemy, you will get stronger and stronger, and he will get weaker and weaker.

What demons cannot handle is a long war. They want you to hit them and give up. But you have the mentality that you will continue in prayer, fasting, and putting pressure on this demon, because it is just a matter of time before it breaks!

Sometimes you have to weaken demons. We have experienced this in our deliverance ministry at Crusaders Church. We've dealt with demons that are very strong. Over a period of time we will pray, fast, rebuke, and hold several sessions dealing with the same demon, but after a while we'll see that demon getting weaker and weaker.

When you first start praying for deliverance from some demonic spirits, they will tell you, "We aren't going. You can't cast us out. You don't have power. We're going to stay here. We are going to destroy. You belong to us. This is our house." You just say, "OK. Just keep talking. I'm going to pray—pray in tongues, fast, rebuke the devil, plead the blood, quote scriptures..." Then after a while those same tough-talking demons will say, "Would you leave us alone? Would you give it a break? You are getting on our nerves."

You can always tell when demons are starting to weaken, because they get angry and start threatening. They'll say, "We're going to kill you." Don't be afraid. That's called panic. When you start seeing the devil panic, you know that you need to keep putting on the pressure until he whimpers out of your life.

Just because it's a long war does not mean you are losing. People have asked me why God would allow certain things to stay in our lives for long periods of time. God allows it because He wants to teach us how to fight. You learn faith and persistence in long war. You need that as a child of God. You need to learn how to stand in faith against impossible situations. You don't look at how it looks. You need to believe God.

When God sent Israel into the land to drive out the enemy, God didn't let them drive all the enemies out of the land in one year. Judges 3:2 says that God left some of the nations in Canaan to teach Israel how to fight. Many of the ones that came out of Egypt knew nothing about warfare.

Sometimes as you are battling darkness, the Lord is teaching you how to war, how to use your faith, how to use the Word, how to use prayer, and how to stand. He wants to teach you how to fight so you will not be a wimp in the army of the Lord. The greatest warriors in God's kingdom are people who have had to fight battles for themselves and overcome some things. When you overcome stuff, it is no longer a theory from the Bible. You know victory is real, and you know how to achieve it. That gives you a much better ability to fight for other people, to use your faith, and to develop your strength in the Lord.

A lot of believers don't like a long war. They give up. This is what the enemy is counting on. He is hoping the people of God will get tired and quit. What he wants us to feel is that we can't do it, that we can't defeat him, and that we won't win. He wants to bluff us that we are not strong enough. But I say to you, don't give up. Don't roll over and die. If God be for you, who can be against you (Rom. 8:31)? God is on your side. You may have to fight for what's yours, and it may take some time. But when you pray and fast and commit to seeing victory no matter how long it takes, it is only a matter of time until the enemy will break, and you will have victory.

—JOHN ECKHARDT, *DELIVERANCE AND SPIRITUAL WARFARE MANUAL*

DATE:

WHAT IS THE LORD SPEAKING TO YOU?

_____

_____

_____

_____

_____

_____

_____

_____

_____

_____

_____

> Then they cried out to the LORD in their
> trouble, and He brought out of their dis-
> tress. He made the storm to be calm, and
> the waves of the sea were hushed.
>
> —PSALM 107:28–29

_____

_____

_____

_____

_____

_____

_____

_____

_____

BATTLE PLANS AND BREAKTHROUGHS

WHAT IS THE LORD SPEAKING TO YOU?

_____

_____

_____

_____

_____

_____

_____

_____

_____

_____

But He said to me, "My grace is suffi-
cient for you, for My strength is made perfect in weakness." Therefore most gladly
I will boast in my weaknesses, that the
power of Christ may rest upon me.

—2 CORINTHIANS 12:9

_____

_____

_____

_____

_____

_____

_____

_____

_____

BATTLE PLANS AND BREAKTHROUGHS

DATE:

WHAT IS THE LORD SPEAKING TO YOU?

_____

_____

_____

_____

_____

_____

_____

_____

_____

_____

_____

> Hide me from the secret schemes of the
> wicked, from the turmoil of the workers of
> iniquity, who sharpen their tongues like a
> sword, and aim bitter words like arrows, that
> they may shoot in secret at the blameless; sud-
> denly they shoot at him and do not fear.
>
> —PSALM 64:2–4

_____

_____

_____

_____

_____

_____

_____

_____

_____

BATTLE PLANS AND BREAKTHROUGHS

WHAT IS THE LORD SPEAKING TO YOU?

_____

_____

_____

_____

_____

_____

_____

_____

_____

_____

And he shall say to them, "Hear, O Israel, you approach today to do battle against your enemies. Do not be fainthearted. Do not fear, and do not tremble or be terrified because of them. For the LORD your God is He that goes with you, to fight for you against your enemies, to save you."

—DEUTERONOMY 20:3–4

_____

_____

_____

_____

_____

_____

_____

_____

_____

BATTLE PLANS AND BREAKTHROUGHS

WHAT IS THE LORD SPEAKING TO YOU?

When the wicked came against me to devour my flesh—my enemies and my foes—they stumbled and fell. Though an army may encamp against me, my heart will not fear; though war may rise against me, yet I will be confident.

—PSALM 27:2–3

_____

_____

_____

_____

_____

_____

_____

_____

_____

BATTLE PLANS AND BREAKTHROUGHS

WHAT IS THE LORD SPEAKING TO YOU?

_____

_____

_____

_____

_____

_____

_____

_____

_____

_____

And he said, "Pay attention all Judah, and
those dwelling in Jerusalem, and King
Jehoshaphat: Thus says the LORD to you, 'Do
not fear, nor be dismayed because of this great
army, for the battle is not yours, but God's.'"

—2 CHRONICLES 20:15

_____

_____

_____

_____

_____

_____

_____

_____

_____

BATTLE PLANS AND BREAKTHROUGHS

WHAT IS THE LORD SPEAKING TO YOU?

_____

_____

_____

_____

_____

_____

_____

_____

_____

_____

"It will not be necessary for you to fight in this conflict. Take your positions, stand, and observe the deliverance of the LORD for you, O Judah and Jerusalem." Do not fear or be filled with terror. Tomorrow, go out before them, and the LORD will be with you.

—2 CHRONICLES 20:17

_____

_____

_____

_____

_____

_____

_____

_____

_____

BATTLE PLANS AND
BREAKTHROUGHS

WHAT IS THE LORD SPEAKING TO YOU?

_____

_____

_____

_____

_____

_____

_____

_____

_____

_____

_____

When the tempest passes, the wicked is no
more, but the righteous stands firm forever.

—PROVERBS 10:25

_____

_____

_____

_____

_____

_____

_____

_____

_____

_____

BATTLE PLANS AND BREAKTHROUGHS

WHAT IS THE LORD SPEAKING TO YOU?

_____

_____

_____

_____

_____

_____

_____

_____

_____

_____

_____

The LORD is on my side; I will not
fear. What can man do to me?

—PSALM 118:6

_____

_____

_____

_____

_____

_____

_____

_____

_____

_____

BATTLE PLANS AND
BREAKTHROUGHS

WHAT IS THE LORD SPEAKING TO YOU?

_____

_____

_____

_____

_____

_____

_____

_____

_____

_____

_____

> Truly I say to you, if you have faith as a grain
> of mustard seed, you will say to this moun-
> tain, "Move from here to there," and it will
> move. And nothing will be impossible for you.
>
> —MATTHEW 17:20

_____

_____

_____

_____

_____

_____

_____

_____

_____

_____

BATTLE PLANS AND BREAKTHROUGHS

DATE:

WHAT IS THE LORD SPEAKING TO YOU?

_____

_____

_____

_____

_____

_____

_____

_____

_____

_____

Plead my cause, O LORD, with those
who contend with me; fight against
those who fight against me!

—PSALM 35:1

196

_____

_____

_____

_____

_____

_____

_____

_____

_____

BATTLE PLANS AND
BREAKTHROUGHS

WHAT IS THE LORD SPEAKING TO YOU?

_____

_____

_____

_____

_____

_____

_____

_____

_____

_____

I have told you these things so that in
Me you may have peace. In the world
you will have distress. But be of good
cheer. I have overcome the world.

—JOHN 16:33

_____

_____

_____

_____

_____

_____

_____

_____

_____

BATTLE PLANS AND
BREAKTHROUGHS